Her Excellency

A Play in Two Acts by

Louis E.V. Nevaer

Based on a true arms-for-hostages scandal

Publication date: September 2014

ISBN 978-1-939879-14-1

Contact publisher for additional copies and performance rights information:

Hispanic Economics, Inc.
P.O. Box 140681
Coral Gables, FL 33114-0681
info@hispaniceconomics.com

Cover and interior design by John Clifton
johnclifton.net

DEDICATION

For Marcia Bosshardt and Mark Cullinane who, as their guest at the U.S. Embassy in Managua, inspired me to tell this story.

SYNOPSIS

The arms-for-hostages scandal casts a shadow over Ronald
Reagan's foreign policy. Jeane Kirkpatrick, American
ambassador to the United Nations, is in conflict with Nora
Astorga, Nicaragua's deputy foreign minister who has
become that nation's ambassador to the United Nations. The
women, mocked as "Amazonian Bitches" by the delegates to
this male-dominated organization, clash ideologically as
each tries to sway world public opinion. Their confrontations
become legendary as they work feverishly to prevail—each
coming to respect the other before fate intervenes.

CAST OF CHARACTERS

JEANE KIRKPATRICK, U.S. ambassador to the United Nations

CHARLES REYNOLDS, her aide

NORA ASTORGA, Nicaraguan ambassador to the United Nations

CARLOS GONZÁLEZ, her aide

RONALD REAGAN, President of the United States

NANCY REAGAN, his wife

SETTING

The action takes place in offices in New York City and Washington, D.C. from 1984 to 1988.

A single unit set, comprised of two offices in the United Nations building, the Oval Office at the White House, the women's room at the United Nations, and an office at the American Enterprise Institute. These locations are in separate areas of the stage, allowing the various scenes to flow immediately from one to the other.

SYNOPSIS OF SCENES

Act I

Scene 1

United Nations. New York.

1984. Jeane KIRKPATRICK, *a woman in her late 50s, stands before a mirror in her office located in the United Nations building in New York. She is putting on earrings and straightening her jacket. Charles* REYNOLDS, *her aide, is in the office with her. There is an American flag, a framed photograph of President* RONALD REAGAN, *and the seal of the United Nations on the wall. The two are engaged in conversation prior to a meeting of the United Nations Security Council.*

KIRKPATRICK. How do you say "bitch" in Spanish, Charles? You're the kind to know these things.

REYNOLDS. I believe the word is "perra," Madam Ambassador.

KIRKPATRICK. Peh-rah?

REYNOLDS. Yes, but not quite.

KIRKPATRICK. Oh, not quite how?

REYNOLDS. Peh-rrrah, rather than peh-rah.

KIRKPATRICK. Isn't that what I said, peh-rah?

REYNOLDS. You said "peh-rah" when it should be closer to "peh-rrrah."

KIRKPATRICK. Is my "rah" off?

REYNOLDS. In Spanish, Madam Ambassador, a double r is pronounced "rrrrr." It rolls off the tongue.

KIRKPATRICK. The way Ricky Ricardo spoke on *I Love Lucy*, then?

REYNOLDS. Yes, something like that.

KIRKPATRICK. Well, I'm not sure I'll be able to do that, speak like Ricky Ricardo singing "Babalu" or something. *(There is a pause as she straightens her jacket.)* That's an odd word, "Babalu."

REYNOLDS. "Babalu" is not a word; it's a name.

KIRKPATRICK. A name?

REYNOLDS. Babalu is a deity in the Afro-Cuban religion of Santería.

KIRKPATRICK. Stop. Please stop. I'm not interested in cluttering my mind with shit. *(There is a pause as she picks up lipstick.)* Peh-rah. *(There is a pause.)* Peh-rah. Peh-rah. *(There is a pause.)* Is that better, Charles?

REYNOLDS. I'm afraid it isn't. "Peh-rah" with a soft r means "pear." "Peh-rrrah" with a rolling r means "bitch." You're saying "pear," not "bitch."

KIRKPATRICK. Damn, I hate languages. Ironic that I'm in a wretched building where there are some 185 or so recognized languages, isn't it?

REYNOLDS. One could say that, I suppose.

KIRKPATRICK. Suppose? Do you suppose if I practice a bit more I would be able to pronounce it properly? I do want to be prepared when I meet Nicaragua's envoy, that bitch.

REYNOLDS. Practice makes perfect, they say.

KIRKPATRICK. Yes, but they also say things happen for a reason, and often fail to mention that the reason is stupid, or arbitrary, or immaterial. *(She puckers her lips as she applies the lip gloss. She stares intently at her image. There is a slight pause.)* Peh-rah. Peh-rrah. Peh-rrrah.

REYNOLDS. Much better, Madam Ambassador! Much better by far!

KIRKPATRICK. Good. It's reassuring to know I can get things right if I set my mind to it, Charles! Now, where is the folder with the notes over this Security Council meeting? I'm not interested in anything Schultz at State has to say about it; I'm just interested in the White House's stance.

REYNOLDS. Yes, I'll get the most recent comments from the White House.

(REYNOLDS *exits.* KIRKPATRICK *continues to practice saying "bitch" in Spanish, her confidence growing as she puts the finishing touches on her makeup.*)

KIRKPATRICK. Peh-rrrah! Peh-rrah! No, that last one was not right. "She's a bitch." "Es una peh-rah." No, that's not right. "She's a bitch," not "She's a pear." I can't very well insult that bitch by calling her a pear. Peh-rrah! Peh-rrrah! Peh-rrrrah! That's it! Es una perra! Una perra es! She's a bitch! A bitch she is! Es una perra!

(REYNOLDS *enters. He clears his throat.*)

REYNOLDS. The notes, Madam Ambassador.

KIRKPATRICK. Yes, of course. Have you ever thought about teaching languages, Charles? (*In a lighthearted manner*) I ask because it seems to me you are a natural born teacher. I mean, look at the way that, without much effort, you educated me about the difference between saying "pear" and "bitch" in Spanish. It's a natural gift, this way with languages.

REYNOLDS. Thank you for the compliment.

KIRKPATRICK. Nonsense, Charles. It's not a compliment. It is an affirmation of reality. (*There is a pause.*) Now, what is the strategy for a counter-argument to the French? To think of the monumental effort we expended saving them during World War II only to have to fight them on every damn point about every damn thing at the United Nations! I'd ask you how to say "ungrateful" in French, but one foreign language lesson is enough for one day.

REYNOLDS. Of course. (*There is a pause as he goes through the notes.*) The White House's comments are not so much about the French as about the Germans. Germany is very receptive to Nicaragua's concerns about the U.S. supplying weapons to the Contras.

KIRKPATRICK. The Germans, now there's a study in reverse Darwinism if there ever was one. To think that a couple of generations ago the Germans had balls. Make no mistake, the desire to take over the entire world, now that's ambition. And look at the German nation today? Apologizing for this, apologizing for that. Sensitive to this concern, sensitive to that concern. Pacifist hippies in the late sixties was the worse we ever got to that wretched mentality in our country, Charles. But to look at the Germans today is to behold a nation of eunuchs! No balls! Absolutely no balls! Germany is a cautionary tale that the Democrats should always keep in mind, with their tendency of always blaming the United States first when it comes to about everything. See what beating themselves up over Hitler has done to Germany? They've gone from being a nation of great men to a nation of limp-dick pacifists. It's painful to see such a thing. The once proud Germans are nothing more than whimpering eunuchs. No balls.

REYNOLDS. Would you like to know the word for balls in Spanish, Madam Ambassador?

(She looks at him with a mock smile.)

KIRKPATRICK. That won't be necessary, Charles. I'm happy to be able to say, "Es una perra"—and I will be happier still when I can say it to that bitch's face and in her damn language! *(She turns to him.)* Now, how is this? "Nora Astorga es una perra!"

REYNOLDS. That's excellent!

KIRKPATRICK. Gracias, Charles.

REYNOLDS. See? You can teach an old dog a new trick!

(She looks at him with a stern expression.)

KIRKPATRICK. Watch it, Charles!

Scene 2

United Nations, New York.

Nora ASTORGA, *a woman in her mid-30s, smartly attired in her "dress for success" outfit, is in her office at the United Nations. There is the Nicaraguan flag, a framed photograph of President Daniel Ortega, and the seal of the United Nations on the wall. There are floral arrangements everywhere. She is going through a box of documents with her aide, Carlos* GONZÁLEZ, *who is confined to a wheelchair. The two are discussing the transition in Nicaragua's representation before the world body.*

GONZÁLEZ. One would think that Cinderella had stepped into the room and all the princes were clamoring for your favors, Nora.

ASTORGA. Now, Carlos, let's not be dramatic.

GONZÁLEZ. I'm a mild-mannered diplomat, not a man prone to exaggeration. Look around you—this office looks more like a florist shop than a diplomatic mission. The flowers have not stopped arriving since it was confirmed you would be here. The French, German, Italian, Spanish, Greek, Japanese, Mexican, and Indian missions have all sent floral arrangements. The list of ambassadors who want to meet with you is three times as long.

ASTORGA. We both know they are more interested in the notoriety of my past than in the work at hand.

GONZÁLEZ. Perhaps. The Reagan administration is furious that, after rejecting you as ambassador to Washington, you suddenly find yourself in New York at the United Nations and directing a lawsuit against the U.S. at The Hague.

ASTORGA. I hope the notoriety wears off. Remember, my chief objective is to prevail over the United States at the World Court. Nicaragua needs to be compensated for the Americans mining our harbors in violation of international law. Winning at the World Court is the only thing that interests me right now.

GONZÁLEZ. Oh, yes, that reminds me. The French ambassador wants to take you to lunch at Le Cirque at your earliest convenience to reiterate that Paris is prepared to send a team of experts to clear the mines in Managua's harbor at any moment.

ASTORGA. He is a charmer, isn't he?

GONZÁLEZ. I believe the charmer is you.

ASTORGA. Is that so?

GONZÁLEZ. Yes, it is so. You know what they call you?

ASTORGA. *(She walks to the various floral arrangements, reading the cards.)* I can only imagine. In recent years, I have been called many things.

GONZÁLEZ. Well, today, at the United Nations, you are called Nora Notorious.

ASTORGA. *(Laughing)* Notorious?

GONZÁLEZ. Yes, you are Nora Notorious.

ASTORGA. Do you suppose that's the case?

GONZÁLEZ. It all depends on one's political persuasion. The Cuban ambassador has seldom walked with as much pride, reminding everyone that thousands of Cuban doctors are everywhere in Nicaragua providing medical attention to millions who went without any medical care while the U.S.-backed dictator siphoned millions to his bank accounts in Miami.

ASTORGA. Is that so?

GONZÁLEZ. The Mexican ambassador continues to remind everyone that Mexico is host to the Contadora Group—and is working to broker a peace settlement for the whole of Central America.

ASTORGA. Now, Carlos, that news is, in its own way, rather amusing. But inconsequential posturing aside, we have to be precise on my presence here, our task, and the focus of our work. I am, technically, the Deputy Foreign Minister, although I will assume the greater role of acting ambassador. My principle objective is the case against the United States at the World Court.

Then it is to present Nicaragua's position before the world community. I don't expect that my official appointment as ambassador to the United Nations will be finalized for another year. We have to allow enough time to pass, since the U.S. refused to accept me as ambassador to Washington. Then my appointment here will not be seen as a provocation to the United States.

GONZÁLEZ. Well, notorious is what they are saying, Nora. They're saying your presence is a direct challenge to the Reagan administration.

ASTORGA. I know. *(She walks around, smelling this flower and that flower.)* It would be dishonest of me to say that there is not an element of payback to the White House, but such is the nature of life.

GONZÁLEZ. What about ... her?

ASTORGA. What about her?

GONZÁLEZ. She has shown nothing but outrage ever since it was disclosed that Nicaragua v. U.S. was to be heard by the World Court. And she went ballistic when she was told that you were coming to the United Nations. Everyone knows she met three times with the Secretary-General, our dear Javier, to discuss the U.N. rejecting your credentials.

ASTORGA. I'm aware of the situation.

GONZÁLEZ. That aside, now, have you also considered the logistics?

ASTORGA. Logistics?

GONZÁLEZ. There are almost two hundred delegations accredited to the United Nations, Nora. Of those, fewer than half a dozen are headed by women.

ASTORGA. Is this your way of telling me this is a male-dominated or sexist institution?

GONZÁLEZ. Misogyny is a given, of course, Nora. What I am referring to is . . .

ASTORGA. Is what? Speak up, Carlos. Say whatever it is you're trying to say!

GONZÁLEZ. There's only one restroom for female

ambassadors. You will be running into Jeane
Kirkpatrick in the women's room all the time—every
day!

ASTORGA. *(She laughs.)* As if that had taken up much of my
time, thinking about the restrooms! But you're right;
there's only one restroom for women who head
missions here!

GONZÁLEZ. What's so funny about that?

ASTORGA. The idea of Toilet Diplomacy!

GONZÁLEZ. Yes, Toilet Diplomacy.

ASTORGA. I already ran into Ambassador Kirkpatrick, twice.

GONZÁLEZ. It's best you just ignore her, Nora. She's a person
who's just angry at the world for no apparent reason.

ASTORGA. Ignoring her is easier said than done, Carlos. It
seems that our bladders are in sync: Both times I've
seen her have been in the restroom.

GONZÁLEZ. Just ignore her. You know that a caged dog is
not to be feared. And in the kennel that is the United
Nations, she is confined to her office—her cage. She
can bark like a rabid bitch all he wants; it won't make
a difference.

ASTORGA. If it were only that simple! The men want to
amuse themselves watching us claw at each other's
throats. The men here will insist on seeing us not as
their equals, but as two Amazonian warriors fighting,
all for their entertainment.

GONZÁLEZ. Then don't give them that satisfaction.

ASTORGA. *(She picks a flower from one of the bouquets.)*
They think I'm a rare, tropical rose, the simpleton
ambassadors here. They forget that the most precious
rose has the sharpest thorns. My thorns are sharper
than serpent's fangs.

Scene 3

The White House, Washington, D.C.

NANCY REAGAN *and* RONALD REAGAN *are alone in the Oval Office.*

NANCY REAGAN. Do you like my dress? It's new.

RONALD REAGAN. It is?

NANCY REAGAN. Of course it is! It's Oscar de la Renta. This is the first time I'm wearing it! Do you like it?

RONALD REAGAN. I'm sorry, Mommy, but it's just a red dress to me—but it is a very lovely red dress. *(He pauses for a moment before speaking as* NANCY REAGAN *models the dress for him.)* Did you pay for it?

NANCY REAGAN. Of course I did!

RONALD REAGAN. Well, I just want to make sure there's no misunderstanding. You know the ruckus the Democrats caused when you were receiving all these gowns and accessories "on loan."

NANCY REAGAN. Ronnie, don't get me started on that! I was promoting American fashion by accepting gowns and jewelry to wear and show off. It was never my intention to keep any of it! It was all going to be donated to museums and auctions for charity! I saw nothing wrong with it!

RONALD REAGAN. I know, and I don't disagree with you, Mommy. But it was seen as a violation—

NANCY REAGAN. Yes, I know! The Ethics in Government Act! Everything was returned and my press secretary issued the standard "Mrs. Reagan regrets that she failed to heed counsel's advice on the matter," and so on.

RONALD REAGAN. Well, good. As long as you paid for the gown.

NANCY REAGAN. Speaking of press secretaries, I have to tell

you about what just happened.

RONALD REAGAN. What?

NANCY REAGAN. Barbara Bush's press secretary let it be known that Barbara hoped to have more frequent lunches with me. "If the President and Vice President have lunch together every Tuesday, so should the First Lady and Mrs. Bush"—or something to that effect.

RONALD REAGAN. Why, that's not a bad idea.

NANCY REAGAN. It's never going to happen. I can't stand that woman.

RONALD REAGAN. Well, if you had lunch with her more frequently, perhaps you might become better friends.

NANCY REAGAN. It's never going to happen, I said!

RONALD REAGAN. Well, Mommy, think about it.

NANCY REAGAN. No! Just Say No to Barbara Bush is my motto! Besides, it's bullshit about you and George Bush having lunch every Tuesday!

RONALD REAGAN. That's true. We don't have lunch every Tuesday. We try to have lunch every Tuesday— Mexican food here at the White House.

NANCY REAGAN. I know. But the truth is you or he are out of town most Tuesdays, so you only have lunch once a month—twice at most.

RONALD REAGAN. Well, I suppose that's how it turns out to be, the frequency of our lunches.

NANCY REAGAN. Exactly my point! If you and the Vice President only have lunch . . . once a month . . . then Barbara and I should have lunch half as often. Six times a year! No more!

RONALD REAGAN. That doesn't seem often enough.

NANCY REAGAN. Ronnie, I hate that woman. She thinks her family is better than ours. She makes fun of Ron's dancing and Patti's lifestyle choices. As if her children were role models!

RONALD REAGAN. Now, Mommy, you know I never criticize anyone's children. And you have to learn to be more graceful. I remember how you antagonized Barbara when they were nice enough to invite us to Kennebunkport.

NANCY REAGAN. Nice? They had no choice in the matter! For appearances they had to invite us! And we could not refuse. For appearances we had to go!

RONALD REAGAN. But you could have been more gracious. *(Imitating Nancy)* "Is *this* the road George Jr. was pulled over on for drunk driving?" "Oh, is *this* the road George Jr. was pulled on over for drunk driving?"

NANCY REAGAN. Well, I was curious.

RONALD REAGAN. No you weren't! You were trying to ruffle her feathers! There's only one road leading to their compound at Kennebunkport, so we were on the road where he was pulled over for drunk driving all along!

NANCY REAGAN. Well, what of it? George Jr. is an alcoholic. I found out that in 1973 he was arrested for cocaine possession! They had the record expunged, but George Jr. drinks too much and is a cokehead.

RONALD REAGAN. What business is it of yours? It isn't as if that boy has any important responsibilities in this world!

NANCY REAGAN. And that Neil—what a thief! Talk about lack of ethics and dereliction of duty! That savings and loan scandal cost taxpayers untold millions and there he is, going about his life, as if he weren't nothing more than a bandit at the Silverado Savings & Rip-Off! All their children are losers!

RONALD REAGAN. Enough!

NANCY REAGAN. Well, they are losers!

RONALD REAGAN. You know that's not true.

NANCY REAGAN. Yes. I forgot. Robin Bush. She's not a loser—because she had the good sense to die before reaching the age of four! She knew she was destined to be raised by that harpy—and she decided to check out at once.

RONALD REAGAN. Anne Francis Robbins, you stop that right now! *(He pauses.)* I happen to think it is a good idea for you and Barbara to do more things together.

NANCY REAGAN. Well, I don't. And I resent her people
    talking to my people and offering stupid ideas. Do you
    know they suggested that we to go the National Zoo
    and be photographed with the pandas?
RONALD REAGAN. It sounds like a wonderful idea, a great
    photo-op for the magazines and foreign press corps.
NANCY REAGAN. Ronnie! Be reasonable! If I were to go to the
    National Zoo with Barbara Bush there's no guarantee
    that the zookeepers would let her leave! She
    practically belongs in one of the exhibits! I mean, for
    heaven's sake, the difference between Barbara Bush
    and an orangutan is that one wears fake pearls and
    the other doesn't!
RONALD REAGAN. Stop it! That's unkind!
NANCY REAGAN. Well, it's true! Who does that dame think
    she is!
RONALD REAGAN. Don't speak that way! One day you'll blurt
    that out in public, and think of the uproar it will
    cause!
NANCY REAGAN. I don't care!
RONALD REAGAN. Well, you should. Now, I think we should
    both spend more time with the Bushes. I just don't
    understand this animosity of yours toward George and
    Barbara. They're not that bad—they're not
    particularly interesting, but they're passable people.
    They are no different from B-list stars in Hollywood
    we spent decades humoring.
NANCY REAGAN. I just can't help it, Ronnie! You know they
    are both Gemini and I can't get along with anyone
    who's a Gemini!
RONALD REAGAN. Why should that be?
NANCY REAGAN. I don't know! It just is! It's in the stars!
    Barbara was born on June 8 and George was born on
    June 12.
(A buzzer on the President's desk rings.)
RONALD REAGAN. It's my next meeting. Jeane Kirkpatrick is
    here.
NANCY REAGAN. Oh, that woman!

RONALD REAGAN. What? Is Jeane Kirkpatrick also a Gemini?

NANCY REAGAN. No. She's a Sagittarius. But she's *that* kind of a Sagittarius. Not much better.

RONALD REAGAN. Now, Mommy.

NANCY REAGAN. You know full well why I resent that woman! She encouraged you to go along with that "arms for hostages" deal—and it's become a political debacle. Honestly, selling arms to those crazy Persians so Hezbollah would release American hostages—and then sending the proceeds to fund the Contras to overthrow Nicaragua's Sandinista government? And whose idea was it to send Robert McFarlane to Tehran with a birthday cake for the Ayatollah Khomeini? It's all a bunch of shit—and Professor Asshole out there told you it was all a brilliant idea! It is now a full-blown international scandal. The woman's an idiot! Her advice is stupid! You should have listened to George!

RONALD REAGAN. Bush?

NANCY REAGAN. No! George Shultz! George the Gemini is a loser; George the Sagittarius is the smart one that you should listen to.

RONALD REAGAN. Yes, you're right about that; George Shultz did warn me about the potential disaster in trading arms for hostages.

NANCY REAGAN. I know, I know. Kirkpatrick and Shultz are both Sagittarians, but they could not more different! Listen to Shultz and ignore Kirkpatrick!

(The door opens and Jeane KIRKPATRICK *enters.)*

RONALD REAGAN. Jeane, it's good to see you!

KIRKPATRICK. Mr. President, it's good to see you also. Mrs. Reagan.

*(*NANCY REAGAN *ignores* KIRKPATRICK *and addresses the President.)*

NANCY REAGAN. I'll leave you now, Ronnie.

*(*NANCY REAGAN *walks by* KIRKPATRICK. *The women stare at each other.)*

NANCY REAGAN. *(Whispers)* Arms for hostages?

KIRKPATRICK. Gowns for charity?

*(*NANCY REAGAN, *in a huff, walks out and closes the door behind her.)*

RONALD REAGAN. *(Addressing* KIRKPATRICK*)* Now, what's this I hear about an assassin ambassador at the United Nations?

KIRKPATRICK. It's not quite like that, Mr. President. But close enough. Her name is Nora Astorga.

RONALD REAGAN. Nora Astorga?

KIRKPATRICK. The name should sound familiar. The Sandinista regime in Nicaragua wanted to send her as their ambassador to Washington. Her credentials were refused for her role in the assassination of General Reynaldo Pérez Vega.

RONALD REAGAN. Yes, yes, now I remember. It was a provocation by Daniel Ortega, that little dictator, to want to send a murderess to Washington, D.C. And now, she's going to serve at the United Nations? Have you spoken to the Secretary-General?

KIRKPATRICK. Yes, I have, Mr. President. Secretary-General Javier Pérez de Cuéllar informed me that if she is the envoy Nicaragua wants to send to the United Nations, then the world body will have no objections to her appointment. He also reminded me that, at present, she is Deputy Foreign Minister. I reminded him, however, that for all intents and purposes, she will be acting ambassador.

RONALD REAGAN. How can that be? How can she just saunter on in and assume the role of an ambassador to the U.N.? This woman is a confessed assassin! That alone makes her unfit to serve; she has no morals.

KIRKPATRICK. I made that point to Pérez de Cuéllar as well, Mr. President. "If we ban individuals based on their moral character," he said, "then this building would be empty."

RONALD REAGAN. He's got a point there. But her role in the killing of that general rises to the level of a war crime, doesn't it? He was a CIA agent and the right-hand man to Anastasio Somoza, an ally of the United States of America.

KIRKPATRICK. Well, Pérez de Cuéllar insisted that if the United Nations started to ban people based on the fact that they may be considered unindicted war criminals, it would be difficult to know where to draw the line.

RONALD REAGAN. Meaning what?

KIRKPATRICK. Meaning that the U.N. would ban Henry Kissinger, since many member states consider him to be an unindicted war criminal. Can you imagine?

RONALD REAGAN. Henry? Sweet Henry who drools all over himself when he speaks?

KIRKPATRICK. Yes, Mr. President. Henry Kissinger. *That* Henry.

RONALD REAGAN. An unindicted war criminal? I don't understand. He won the Nobel Peace Prize!

KIRKPATRICK. That means nothing; the Nobel Peace Prize has been awarded to all kinds of people—including terrorists. Remember, Menachem Begin, while a freedom fighter in 1946, carried out the bombing of the King David Hotel in Jerusalem. Ninety-one people were killed in what today is considered to have been a terrorist attack on the British. Then, decades later, in 1979, he shared the Nobel Peace Prize with Anwar Sadat. That's how the world works; one day you're a terrorist bombing hotels and killing men, women, and children; the next day you're accepting a peace prize in Sweden before the world community.

RONALD REAGAN. So Nora Astorga is headed for the United Nations one way or another. *(He pauses and reflects.)* In short, you're certain to have to deal with a murderess.

KIRKPATRICK. That would appear to be that case. And I have to be honest with you, Mr. President. I hate that woman. She's an assassin, a Communist, anti-American, and—most damning of all—she's a bitch. Any woman, in my opinion, who would use her sex the way she did is beneath contempt and a bitch.

RONALD REAGAN. Well, Jeane, you are going to have to work with her, bitch or not, however best you can.

KIRKPATRICK. I'm prepared to resign in protest, Mr. President.

RONALD REAGAN. Jeane, I won't allow that.

KIRKPATRICK. I just don't know what course of action would be principled other than my resignation in protest. The idea that one of my so-called "colleagues" at the United Nations killed an ally of the United States is enough to make me sick.

RONALD REAGAN. I can understand your reaction, but I am not prepared to accept your resignation. Nancy and I spoke about this. So I'm going to give you her and my advice.

KIRKPATRICK. *(Surprised)* Mrs. Reagan has advice for me?

RONALD REAGAN. Yes, she does. Nancy said that you and Nora Astorga are both Sagittarians—and that, by nature, you are both fiery and combative. She also said that the two of you will be able to work together because pragmatism prevails in the professional lives of those born under the sign of Sagittarius.

KIRKPATRICK. That's Mrs. Reagan's advice?

RONALD REAGAN. It is—and mine is a slight variation of it, Jeane. When it comes to you and Nora Astorga, I'm going to give you exactly the same advice that I give Nancy when it comes to Barbara Bush. So listen closely now: When it comes to Nora Astorga, you are just going to have to *suck it up.*

Scene 4

United Nations, New York.

Jeane KIRKPATRICK *and her aide, Charles* REYNOLDS, *are at their offices at the United Nations.* KIRKPATRICK *has returned from Washington, D.C., and is developing strategies on how to undermine the impact that Nora* ASTORGA'S *presence is having on the influence of the United States at the U.N.*

KIRKPATRICK. It has come to this, Charles?

REYNOLDS. What has, Madam Ambassador?

KIRKPATRICK. The art of sucking up. I mean the way these ambassadors are fawning over that Killer Bitch, Nora Astorga. One would think she was a Hollywood celebrity! Who would have thought there would come a day when we'd have celebrity politicians? People in office who entertain but do not govern?

REYNOLDS. You're right on that point, Madam Ambassador. It's odd, the lack of decorum when things become a question of celebrity. I remember how there was such concern that the Reagans would turn the White House into Hollywood East, but that never happened. The Reagans kept the separation of politics and entertainment in check.

KIRKPATRICK. Precisely! The separation of Church and State. The separation of Public Policy and Public Entertainment! You'd never imagine Ronald Reagan signing a duet with Frank Sinatra at the White House. But Washington, D.C. is far different from the United Nations. That woman's impact on the United Nations is like . . . like . . .

REYNOLDS. . . . like performance art by one of Andy Warhol's groupies!

KIRKPATRICK. Precisely, Charles! It's diplomacy as performance art! It's international affairs as a sixties-style happening, or whatever nonsense Warhol and his strung out band of loser groupies used to call their degenerate carryings-on!

REYNOLDS. You know what they say, there's no accounting for taste.

KIRKPATRICK. Is that what they say, Charles?

REYNOLDS. Yes, they do. But in this case, it is her notoriety that captivates the imagination of the ambassadors. She enters the delegates' lounge and a path opens before her, like the Red Sea parting. She has all the members of the Non-Aligned Movement lining up to kiss her on both cheeks and proffering luncheon invitations to consult on this matter and to confer on that issue. She has them all enchanted with her wit and charm. That's reason enough for you to, perhaps, well . . . it would behoove you to venture into the delegates' lounge.

KIRKPATRICK. I most certainly will not! You know my feelings about the United Nations, Charles. Never in my life have I been subjected to such rank sexism as I have here in the confines of this institution! I am not about to enter that room, filled with cigar smoke and men drinking scotch, to compete for their attention— especially when my competitor is that "peh-rrrah" assassin! An affront, such a suggestion, Charles! You know better than that.

REYNOLDS. Outrageous it may very well be, Madam Ambassador, but it does put you at a strategic and competitive disadvantage when making the American case before the world community. There's no denying she's like a goddess, with her classic features and flawless complexion. All heads turn to watch her whenever she enters the room . . .

KIRKPATRICK. Yes, I know.

REYNOLDS. And have you seen the bouquets of flowers? Dozens of delegations sent her floral arrangements. I walked by the Nicaraguan office and there were eleven—I counted them—floral arrangements on two tables outside. The custodial staff had to bring up two folding tables because there are so many bouquets that there was no place for them in her office.

KIRKPATRICK. That miserable bitch. How can the United States compete against someone whose very presence electrifies these asshole ambassadors—who have shit for brains? And she knows what she's doing. I've seen her reach for a glass of water when we're in conference. The moment her hand moves, eyes begin to turn to her, and when she senses their attention, she crosses her legs, and the conference room stops. You'd think she wasn't wearing underwear!

REYNOLDS. You do know she's compared to biblical characters, Madam Ambassador?

KIRKPATRICK. Oh, so now the Bible is involved?

REYNOLDS. Yes, it is.

KIRKPATRICK. The Bible?

REYNOLDS. In the Book of Judges, Jael is praised for her righteousness when she murders the Canaanite general Sisera. After General Sisera saw his forces slain by the Israelites, Jael invited the general into her husband's tent, offered him a blanket to warm himself, and calmed his shattered nerves by offering warm milk. When the general fell asleep, Jael drove a stake through his forehead. Then she proudly announced her murder of the hated enemy of Israel to everyone who would listen. Jael was guilty of the deadly sin of Pride—and for that, she is held as righteous! Nora Astorga is seen as a modern-day Jael.

KIRKPATRICK. Is that what they are saying about this Killer Bitch?

REYNOLDS. From memory, Book of Judges 4:21, "Then Jael Heber's wife took a nail of the tent, and took an hammer in her hand, and went softly unto him, and smote the nail into his temples, and fastened it into the ground: for he was fast asleep and weary. So he died." King James Bible.

KIRKPATRICK. King James Bible?

REYNOLDS. Yes. King James Bible.

KIRKPATRICK. I just don't understand, Charles, how, in that

head of yours, you manage to store so much shit! *(She pauses, then turns to the mirror.)* The Holy Bible. Do you see the state of the world today, Charles? Nora Astorga, that Killer Bitch, is being compared to something out of the Holy Land. Holy fuck! *(She straightens her jacket, then looks down.)*

REYNOLDS. What's wrong?

KIRKPATRICK. What do you mean? Nothing's wrong.

REYNOLDS. Madam Ambassador, I've known you too long to know when something is not right.

KIRKPATRICK. Do you? Do you know me that well, Charles?

REYNOLDS. Yes, I do.

KIRKPATRICK. Oh, all right. Bullshit biblical references aside, Charles, what I find perplexing is that it would be simple to dismiss her as an empty-headed woman of no consequence. But I can't. I've read the legal arguments she is preparing in Nicaragua's suit against the U.S. at the World Court. And they are astonishing. That woman possesses a brilliant legal mind! She is constructing a case against us like a Swiss watchmaker assembles a timepiece.

REYNOLDS. I see. I understand the conflict you face.

KIRKPATRICK. Conflict? Whatever do you mean?

REYNOLDS. The conflict of emotions, Madam Ambassador. You hate her, but not entirely. Because you respect her intellect.

KIRKPATRICK. That's not it!

REYNOLDS. Of course it is! And it's perfectly understandable. If one can have dictatorships and double standards, why can't one have enemies and conflicted passions?

KIRKPATRICK. Oh, you're good, Charles! You're good. No wonder I keep you around!

REYNOLDS. Thank you, Madam Ambassador. Now, what shall we do about the flowers?

KIRKPATRICK. Flowers?

REYNOLDS. Yes. The United States of America cannot ignore Nora Astorga by not sending her office a token of friendship to welcome her to the United Nations.

Especially when so many other countries have been so extravagant in showing their affection for her. In a word: flowers.

KIRKPATRICK. Flowers? From me? No, that will never do, Charles. But you're right. We have to send that peh-rrrah something. Otherwise, innumerable cables will be sent to capitals around the world claiming that the U.S. snubbed Nicaragua. And we can't have that.

REYNOLDS. If not flowers, then what?

KIRKPATRICK. Oh, I'll think of something apropos to the occasion, Charles. I'll come up with the perfect gift for a peh-rrrah.

Scene 5

United Nations, New York.

Nora ASTORGA *is in her office with her aide, Carlos* GON-
ZÁLEZ. *The two are discussing the World Court.*

GONZÁLEZ. The arguments at the World Court are going
very well. The consensus is that a ruling will favor us
and the court will order the United States to
compensate Nicaragua.

ASTORGA. Then this means we have to work even harder if
victory is not to slip through our fingers. *(She notices
a fruit basket on her desk.)* What's this?

GONZÁLEZ. The Americans sent that to you.

(She walks over and picks up the card.)

ASTORGA. It's from Ambassador Kirkpatrick.

GONZÁLEZ. Read it.

(She opens the card and reads it.)

ASTORGA. "I look so forward to rigorous debate about ideas,
Ms. Astorga. Welcome to the United Nations. Jeane
Kirkpatrick."

*(*GONZÁLEZ *shrugs his shoulders as the two look at each
other.)*

GONZÁLEZ. Fruit, not flowers?

ASTORGA. Yes, but why would she send me a basket of
pears?

Scene 6

The White House, Washington, D.C.

NANCY REAGAN *and* RONALD REAGAN *are alone in the Oval Office, 1985.*

NANCY REAGAN. The legacy of the Reagan foreign policy has been undermined by this arms-for-hostages disaster, Ronnie. Something dramatic has to be done. Something that will be a game changer—and become part of your legacy.

RONALD REAGAN. You're right about that, Mommy. I just wish this Iran-Contra scandal weren't so infuriating. How the media love to mock me as the "Teflon President," but this is one mistake that is sticking to me personally, and I don't like it.

NANCY REAGAN. Neither do I, which is why I consulted my astrological adviser. We've found the solution, Ronnie.

RONALD REAGAN. The solution?

NANCY REAGAN. Yes. This administration has to win a definitive victory in America's dealings with the Soviet Union, even if I hate that Russian bitch, Raisa Gorbachev. That woman is the most disagreeable Capricorn I have ever met in my life! I'd like to ram a goat's horn up her ass!

RONALD REAGAN. Mommy, be nice! Now, that aside, I know Mikhail Gorbachev has placed a great deal of hope on his glasnost—but I don't think we can have much of an influence in the reforms now underway. I'd always hoped that we could make a breakthrough on reaching an Intermediate-Range Nuclear Forces Treaty.

NANCY REAGAN. It can be done. It may take time, but the foundation has to be established correctly.

RONALD REAGAN. Foundation? A foundation for reaching an arms agreement?

NANCY REAGAN. Yes! We need to have a foreign policy victory to balance out the Iran-Contra scandal. I've researched this, Ronnie. Hear me out: Mikhail Gorbachev is a Pisces, born on March 2nd. That makes him the kind of person that will meet you halfway—and I mean that in a literal sense.

RONALD REAGAN. A literal sense?

NANCY REAGAN. Ronnie, if you travel to Moscow or he travels to Washington, the talks will not progress. You and he must meet halfway . . . in order to begin the process of reaching a compromise.

RONALD REAGAN. Halfway?

NANCY REAGAN. When dealing with a Pisces that's the only way to make a go of it. Now, my astrologer and I have surveyed the founding dates of cities throughout Europe. And we have found the answer: Reykjavik!

RONALD REAGAN. Wreck-a-what?

NANCY REAGAN. Reykjavik, the capital of Iceland.

RONALD REAGAN. Iceland?

NANCY REAGAN. Yes, Iceland. Reykjavik is the most auspicious city for holding a conference with Mikhail Gorbachev—and it lies approximately halfway between Moscow and Washington! It was meant to be, don't you see? It is sound astrological foreign policy.

RONALD REAGAN. Iceland? A Reykjavik Summit?

Scene 7

United Nations, New York.

Nora ASTORGA *is in the women's room reserved for female ambassadors. She is wearing a slip and putting on a chic black dress. Gold earrings, a gold bracelet, and a cosmetic bag are on the sink counter. As soon as she finishes putting on the dress and slips into her high heels, the door opens. Jeane* KIRKPATRICK *enters.* ASTORGA *does not turn around but she and* KIRKPATRICK *make eye contact by looking at each other in the mirror.*

ASTORGA. Ambassador Kirkpatrick, good evening.

KIRKPATRICK. Don't speak to me unless I address you first, young woman.

ASTORGA. *(Unfazed, as she puts on earrings.)* We are colleagues, Ambassador Kirkpatrick. And at the United Nations, our countries are equals as well.

KIRKPATRICK. Some are more equal than others.

ASTORGA. Only in an Orwellian world, which this is not.

KIRKPATRICK. My admonishment has nothing to do with our present assignments at this worthless institution, but rather with the disparate levels of our life experiences. I am old enough to be your mother, Nora.

ASTORGA. Nora? Is that the case, Jeane?

KIRKPATRICK. It's Ambassador Kirkpatrick.

ASTORGA. Then I'd appreciate your calling me Deputy Foreign Minister Astorga—until I assume the proper title of Ambassador in a few months.

KIRKPATRICK. That's a fair enough request.

ASTORGA. That's all I, or my country for that matter, want. Fairness.

KIRKPATRICK. Is that so? Tell that to the thousands of families whose livelihoods have been seized by the dictatorship your Sandinista leaders have imposed upon your countrymen.

ASTORGA. Revolutions must find their own way, and one of
our revolution's goals is to achieve a more equitable
distribution of income for the benefit of our people.
The expropriation of wealth accumulated by the
cronies of Anastasio Somoza over the decades they,
with U.S. support, plundered Nicaragua's natural
resources is an act of revolutionary justice. In your
country, American Revolutionaries seized the assets of
those loyal to the British Crown. If our seizure of
assets stolen from the Nicaraguan people offends you,
then perhaps your understanding of what is fair and
just should be reevaluated. Besides, this is not a forum
for discussing any nation's internal affairs.

KIRKPATRICK. Oh, you're good!

(KIRKPATRICK *pauses. She smiles.* ASTORGA *puts on her gold
bracelet, looks herself over in the mirror then reaches
for the cosmetics bag and selects a lipstick.)*

ASTORGA. Why are you staring? Is it because you are not
accustomed to having your political convictions
challenged?

KIRKPATRICK. No, not at all. I have always challenged myself
when it comes to what I believe in terms of politics.
(She smiles and walks closer to ASTORGA, *who is
applying eye shadow.)* A young woman like you looks
at a woman my age and what does she see? Does she
see a maternal figure, or someone who is hopelessly
out of touch? I know what the world sees when they
see me. They see a woman of conviction with strong
political ideas and who doesn't take shit from anyone.

ASTORGA. A Republican hawk, even though you are a
registered Democrat.

KIRKPATRICK. Very good, Deputy Foreign Minister Astorga!
You have done your homework!

ASTORGA. The United States isn't the only country that
compiles dossiers on its . . .

KIRKPATRICK. . . . adversaries?

ASTORGA. And its friends. I'm sure the United States collects as much information on its friends as it does on its adversaries. I wouldn't be surprised if your NSA weren't eavesdropping on the private conversations between Prince Charles and his mistress Camilla Parker Bowles—or Princess Diana and her lover du jour.

KIRKPATRICK. If it is deemed appropriate, I wouldn't doubt it. America's national security is Washington's foremost concern. Now, what else do you know about me that might be surprising to the public at large?

ASTORGA. I'm not sure. It would be presumptuous of me to over- or underestimate the ignorance of the American people.

KIRKPATRICK. My dear, the ignorance of the American electorate can never be underestimated! We are a democracy comprised of functional illiterates—much like the way your country is filled with unschooled peasants!

ASTORGA. How unkind of you.

KIRKPATRICK. What does the truth have to do with kindness? Nothing.

ASTORGA. To answer your question, I do know that you were not always conservative in your political views. I believe you were—would it be correct to characterize you in your youth as socialist?

KIRKPATRICK. My, my! There, there! You are correct! But in my defense, I have to say that youth is a time of misguided optimism and foolish hope. Yes, in my misguided and optimistic youth I was a socialist. My grandfather—D. C. Kirkpatrick—was one of the founding members of the Socialist Party of Oklahoma. No one knows that—at least not in Washington where such information would prove scandalous. And, I must confess, I was very much influenced by him and his optimistic sense of social justice. In fact, during my college freshman year I joined the—

ASTORGA. —Young People's Socialist League.

KIRKPATRICK. Very good! And the Young People's Socialist

League was a wing of the Socialist Party of America. So you see, Deputy Foreign Minister Astorga, as a young woman I went through the same delusional socialist bullshit phase that you—decades my junior—are now meandering through. Which is to say, the conflict that characterizes our nations' relations has more to do with your youthful inexperience about life—as reflected in your naïve political ideology.

ASTORGA. An ideal that one generation fails to achieve does not preclude another generation from being able to realize it.

KIRKPATRICK. *(She laughs.)* And you think that you and your Sandinista dimwits are going to achieve a socialist paradise in Central America? Look at the ruin Fidel Castro has brought on his island nation. What is Cuba if not a white-minority regime ruling over a nation of people of color who live in poverty? In South Africa it's called apartheid. But in Cuba—where's the outcry over a bunch of privileged whites living at the expense of poor people of color? I predict apartheid will long be dismantled before true racial representation takes place in Castro's Island of Doom. And I have no doubt that your Sandinista leadership is dining lavishly tonight while peasants are still barefoot and hungry throughout the whole of Nicaragua.

ASTORGA. If our people are in poverty, it is because our revolution's tasks are made more difficult by your country's hostility by arming the Contras.

KIRKPATRICK. That's bullshit and you know it. The Sandinistas are determined to bring ruin upon your country. *(KIRKPATRICK points to ASTORGA'S dress as she speaks.)* And look at your outfit, my dear. I know Chanel when I see Chanel, even if I would never wear such a thing! How many cans of baby formula could that dress purchase for infants throughout the slums of Managua?

ASTORGA. In the grand scheme of things, my small country's efforts to sway world public opinion when confronted by an aggressive superpower require that I am suited to my role as "ambassador" of the Sandinista revolution before the world community. I have to dress the part. I'm not going out to two events this evening because I want to: I have to in order to represent my country and to stand up for the dignity of my nation.

KIRKPATRICK. "My Country, 'Tis of Thee." Don't be ridiculous! At your age, I, too, loved the nightlife. The wistful philosophical musings of youth! I remember as a college student going to bars with friends to debate philosophy and solve the world's problems. As for you, you're a woman who is about to be toasted—and you relish the attention bestowed upon you! The Canadian ambassador was smart to select Elaine's—it has terrific energy and you'll enjoy it. Yes, we do know your evening's itinerary! That aside, I'm not saying there's anything wrong with your using your femininity to persuade men, but I do think you should be honest and say that you, secretly, delight in how your feminine charms seduce men. You're accomplished with using the power of your sex to entice men, aren't you?

ASTORGA. What do you mean by that?

KIRKPATRICK. I mean nothing by that. It's an observation of fact: You used your feminine charms to lure a man to his death, or are these stories about you mythical?

ASTORGA. I am not ashamed of what happened. And I bear no guilt in the general's death. He was a dog who brutalized my fellow countrymen. Besides, this incident in my life is not nearly as fascinating as understanding the process by which a socialist college student evolved into the conservative hawk standing before me. Was Franz Neumann's influence on you that powerful?

KIRKPATRICK. Professor Neumann! You know about him?

ASTORGA. Franz Neumann, the Revisionist Marxist who was your lead adviser at Columbia University. Yes, I know about him. I can't imagine that he revised Marxism to

such a degree that it led you to be become an adherent
of the radical capitalism of Reaganomics!

KIRKPATRICK. How is such an intellectual journey that much
different from your own? Once upon a time you were a
good Catholic girl, raised with all the comforts a
bourgeois family can provide to their children. You
studied at Catholic University in Washington, D.C.
Then, one fine day, you became a killer and a
revolutionary guerrilla who conspired to overthrow a
government. And now you find yourself as the
propagandist-in-chief to a Marxist revolution! The
actions of the Sandinista regime in Nicaragua only
confirm my contention that Latin America is
pathologically violent. Your own history is testament
to that undeniable fact.

ASTORGA. It is because I was a child of privilege, as you say,
that I was able to see the injustice by which those
privileges were afforded to me!

KIRKPATRICK. Is that what they taught you at Catholic
University? Is that what they teach at the institutions
of higher learning in this country? I doubt they teach
students that they should work to destroy the
socioeconomic system that is able to sustain these very
institutions of higher learning. In all my years as a
professor at Georgetown University, I never taught
my students to overthrow the government! My dear,
young, naïve woman, when a nation turns on its
educated and entrepreneurial classes, as Nicaragua
has, the result is reverse Darwinism—the survival of
the least fit! That's what's happened in Castro's
Cuba—every day, the least fit prevail and society is
diminished. That's why that island is in ruins! Not
because of the U.S. embargo.

ASTORGA. I cannot speak to the Cuban model or experience,
because Nicaragua's revolution reflects the specific
circumstances of my country and our society.
Remember, revolutions are not exportable like Coca-
Cola or paperbacks or something like that. You don't
produce it internally and send it away. Revolutions

are made in a country when the conditions in that
particular country are ripe for a process of change.

KIRKPATRICK. Well, Deputy Foreign Minister Astorga, I hope
that you—as I did—change your views and in short
order. For now, this socialist-turned-capitalist stands
before a capitalist-turned-socialist. Mine is the more
mature path on the road of life. Mine are observations
that a mature woman wishes to impart to the younger
woman standing before her. If your dossier is
complete, you will know that I have always
championed feminist principles and the advancement
of women. In that spirit, I have to be honest with you
and tell you that there is some pride in seeing that
Nicaragua has sent a woman to this body—even if I
find that woman—you—reprehensible.

ASTORGA. Is that a compliment, a convoluted Republican
compliment?

KIRKPATRICK. It is not! I am not a Republican!

ASTORGA. Not yet.

KIRKPATRICK. Not ever! And don't speak back to me that
way, young woman! What kind of nuns taught you
such disrespect? Oh, let me guess, the same fucking
nuns who taught you to slit a man's throat after
luring him to your bedroom!

ASTORGA. That's not how it happened! He was shot.

KIRKPATRICK. Oh, that's a big difference. Did you tell that to
General Pérez Vega's corpse?

ASTORGA. I have to leave now, Ambassador Kirkpatrick.

KIRKPATRICK. I'm sure you do! I can only imagine your
activities after you're done with your professional
engagements this evening. But just remember, Deputy
Foreign Minister Astorga, the moment you step out of
the United Nations building, you will be in New York
City. It's a material world out there. If you're not
prepared to heed the advice of this older and wiser
woman, then avail yourself of the pleadings of that
tawdry chanteuse's song today's misguided youth are
listening to: Embrace the material girl you were

meant to be as your birthright! It's a material world. I'm sure the salesgirls at Chanel endorse my recommendation to you on the matter.

(ASTORGA *picks up her cosmetics bag and moves to the door.* KIRKPATRICK *looks at her.*)

ASTORGA. Good evening, Ambassador Kirkpatrick.

(NORA *exits.* KIRKPATRICK, *alone, smiles.*)

KIRKPATRICK. Nora Astorga. I like this bitch. She's my kind of peh-rrrah.

Act II

Scene 1

The White House. Washington, D.C.

NANCY REAGAN *and* RONALD REAGAN *are alone in the Oval Office.*

NANCY REAGAN. Amazonian bitches. That's what they call them at the United Nations, Jeane Kirkpatrick and Nora Astorga. They are the laughingstock of the U.N., Ronnie. It's the Battle of the Amazonian bitches. To think two women in positions of authority bicker constantly and call each other bitch! I have never heard of such a thing! We've become a joke to the rest of the world!

RONALD REAGAN. How is Barbara Bush?

NANCY REAGAN. What? What made you think of that harpy?

RONALD REAGAN. I don't know. I was hearing you talk and for some reason I thought of Barbara Bush.

NANCY REAGAN. I'm talking about that Latina assassin and Jeane Kirkpatrick. I can't stand that woman! I want Jeane Kirkpatrick out!

RONALD REAGAN. Now, Mommy, Jeane is a very intelligent and effective team player. Why do you resent her so much?

NANCY REAGAN. She treats me as if I'm stupid. As if she was so smart. What infuriates me is that she advised you to go along with that scheme to trade arms for hostages. Anyone with half a brain could tell that those idiots couldn't carry it off without incident. And now it's a scandal. Ronnie, I want her out because she fucked you over!

RONALD REAGAN. No one could have known it would turn into a fiasco—

NANCY REAGAN. That's not true! George Schultz said it was

a terrible idea, and he was right! Only Jeane Kirkpatrick and Caspar Weinberger thought it was a terrific idea. Well, Ronnie, she can fuck with me and I can take it, but when she fucks with you—then that bitch is out!

RONALD REAGAN. Mommy, she's a very good ambassador. I like her.

NANCY REAGAN. Ronnie, you know that I never bring up a problem if I don't offer a solution. Now, hear me out. Nora Astorga is a Sagittarius. Jeane Kirkpatrick is a Sagittarius. That means that in order to maintain an astrological balance at the United Nations, we have to replace Kirkpatrick with the succeeding astrological sign. Does that make sense?

RONALD REAGAN. Well, if you put it that way, I can see the logic of that approach.

NANCY REAGAN. I have the answer! Capricorn follows Sagittarius, so Vernon Walters, who was born on January 3rd, should succeed Jeane Kirkpatrick to become the seventeenth United States Ambassador to the United Nations. It makes perfect astrological sense.

RONALD REAGAN. Why, it does, it does make sense.

NANCY REAGAN. And here's the icing on this payback cake: Vernon Walters is a general!

RONALD REAGAN. And the significance of that?

NANCY REAGAN. Nora Astorga was complicit in the murder of one general, so I'd like to see how she handles *this* general! I'd like to see that Latina assassin slit Vernon Walters' throat!

(The buzzer on RONALD REAGAN'S *desk sounds.)*

RONALD REAGAN. That's Jeane, she's here.

NANCY REAGAN. One more thing. In a few months, when we have a state dinner for Prince Charles and Princess Diana, I want to find a way not to invite the Bushes.

RONALD REAGAN. Now, Nancy, you know we can't do that.

NANCY REAGAN. I just hate the idea of Barbara Bush attending. Did you see her at that ceremony last week? I kept looking back at her, cringing. Her knuckles were practically scrapping along the ground, she's such an ape!

RONALD REAGAN. There's no way we cannot invite them to that state dinner, Mommy.

NANCY REAGAN. Why can't some head of state drop dead a couple of days before—and then you can send the Bushes to represent the U.S. at some funeral?

RONALD REAGAN. Nancy! You can't be hoping some president, premier, or prime minister somewhere dies just because you don't want Barbara Bush to attend a dinner at the White House.

NANCY REAGAN. Well, why not?

(The door opens and KIRKPATRICK *enters.)*

RONALD REAGAN. Because it's not Christian!

NANCY REAGAN. Fuck Christ!

RONALD REAGAN. We'll continue this conversation later. Jeane is here.

*(*NANCY REAGAN *walks to the door, passing* KIRKPATRICK *as she approaches the president's desk.)*

KIRKPATRICK. *(Whispers)* Say hello to Jesus, Mary Magdalene.

*(*RONALD REAGAN *stands to greet* KIRKPATRICK *as they walk to a sitting area.* NANCY REAGAN *slams the door closed on her way out.)*

RONALD REAGAN. Now, Jeane, what's this I hear about our losing support for our policies in Central America? And it's because of that woman, Nora Astorga. What is she like? What can you tell me about her?

KIRKPATRICK. What can I say about her?

RONALD REAGAN. Well, two years ago George Shultz characterized the Sandinistas as a cancer in our landmass. And I'm convinced that Daniel Ortega wishes to use Nicaragua as a platform to allow the Cubans to destabilize neighboring Honduras, El Salvador—and even Guatemala.

KIRKPATRICK. Yes, these revolutionaries are like malignant cells, spreading death in their wake.

RONALD REAGAN. That's why I want to know more about Nora Astorga—the way she charms the other ambassadors is inexplicable—such charisma. What is she like?

KIRKPATRICK. What is she like, Mr. President? *(She pauses, then speaks slowly.)* She wears her past like other women wear perfume.

RONALD REAGAN. I was afraid of that. I was afraid that she'd be—

KIRKPATRICK. —an astonishing creature.

RONALD REAGAN. Is she?

KIRKPATRICK. It's extraordinary to see how she charms the delegates and how sympathetic they are to her. The entire General Assembly believes it is we who are the bullies, working to undermine the new government in Nicaragua. And there is nothing that I can do to stop that perception. It is infuriating!

RONALD REAGAN. Well, Jeane, we are going to have to find a way to neutralize her influence.

KIRKPATRICK. My entire staff is trying to undermine her, but it is an elusive goal, Mr. President. At least for now.

(The door to the office opens and NANCY REAGAN *walks in holding two pieces of dinnerware in her hands.)*

NANCY REAGAN. Oh, I thought you were with nobody, Ronnie. *(She looks over to* KIRKPATRICK.*)* And I see that you are!

KIRKPATRICK. Mrs. Reagan, I'm leaving.

NANCY REAGAN. Good. *(To* RONALD REAGAN.*)* Look at these patterns, Ronnie. They clash! We can't have state dinners with these!

*(*KIRKPATRICK *stands and walks to the door.)*

KIRKPATRICK. *(To* RONALD REAGAN*)* Mr. President, I'll work to limit Nicaragua's influence at the United Nations. If I leave now, I'll be back in New York by dinnertime. *(To* NANCY REAGAN*)* Mrs. Reagan, I'll leave you to solve your . . . umm . . . China crisis.

*(*KIRKPATRICK *smiles as she leaves, closing the door behind her.)*

NANCY REAGAN. I can't stand these women, Ronnie. Jeane
    Kirkpatrick. Barbara Bush. One with fake sentiments,
    the other with fake pearls. There's no difference
    between them. Honestly, Jeane Kirkpatrick is
    Barbara Bush—with brains! That's a frightening
    thought right there!

RONALD REAGAN. Now, Mommy, there you go again, being
    unkind.

NANCY REAGAN. Ronnie, I was being kind! I didn't call either
    woman by their proper names: bitches! They are both
    fucking bitches!

RONALD REAGAN. Nancy!

NANCY REAGAN. Oh, all right! But you promised:
    Kirkpatrick is out, Walters is in! Sagittarius must
    make way for Capricorn!

Scene 2

United Nations, New York.

Nora ASTORGA *is in the women's room reserved for female ambassadors. She is putting on makeup and earrings when Jeane* KIRKPATRICK *enters.* KIRKPATRICK *lights a cigarette.*

ASTORGA. You're smoking? Is smoking allowed in the women's room?

KIRKPATRICK. It is when I light up.

ASTORGA. American exceptionalism?

KIRKPATRICK. Something like that.

ASTORGA. Smoking will give you cancer.

KIRKPATRICK. No it won't. Smoking will give me pleasure. *(She pauses and she offers* ASTORGA *a cigarette.)* I'm sure you've heard by now?

ASTORGA. Heard what?

KIRKPATRICK. The rumors.

ASTORGA. I don't pay attention to rumors.

KIRKPATRICK. In this case, you should. I've been fired.

ASTORGA. You were? I thought you only wanted to serve one term.

KIRKPATRICK. That's the official story, but the truth is that Nancy Reagan had me fired. Retired General Vernon Walters is taking my place. Don't let him bully you, Ambassador Astorga. He's more brawn than brains.

ASTORGA. Are you angry at Mrs. Reagan? *(Pause. She puts out the cigarette.)* She had you fired? What a bitch.

KIRKPATRICK. It's not necessary to state the obvious. Calling Mrs. Reagan a bitch is like calling a cat a feline.

ASTORGA. So those rumors are true. Did they offer you another post?

KIRKPATRICK. They did, but I declined. I've decided to leave government. *(She pauses.)* Now, I've been told you are the guest of the French ambassador and you're having dinner at Union Square Café.

ASTORGA. Yes, it's true.

KIRKPATRICK. New York is abuzz over that twenty-seven-year-old impresario, Danny Meyer. All the critics rave about his restaurant. Enjoy!

ASTORGA. I will.

(KIRKPATRICK *looks at* ASTORGA *for a moment, almost with longing. She puts the cigarette out and speaks.)*

KIRKPATRICK. Women like you don't know what it's like for the rest of us.

ASTORGA. Women like me?

KIRKPATRICK. You're oblivious, aren't you? I'm not surprised. Who can blame the warmth of the tropics for being oblivious to the sting of a winter blizzard?

ASTORGA. What are you talking about?

KIRKPATRICK. My dear, what I mean is that beautiful women are oblivious to the plight of those of us who are not beautiful. You take for granted the attention of men, the way doors are opened, seats offered, gestures of kindness made. But what about the rest of us?

ASTORGA. The rest of you?

KIRKPATRICK. Look at me. I am not now, nor have I ever been, beautiful. I have not ever even been what one might call attractive.

ASTORGA. Nonsense. You look fine to me.

KIRKPATRICK. Fine? A glass of tepid water is also fine. In my youth, at my best, I was never, ever pretty. Plain Jane was a compliment; nondescript was the norm. In my best clothes the most charitable thing that I can be called is dowdy. If my hair is a tad too long, I look like a witch. If it's too short, I look like a dyke.

ASTORGA. You are being ridiculous?

KIRKPATRICK. Am I? Women like me, who are without beauty, have to resort to our intellect to assert ourselves. Ugly women—from Golda Meir to Indira Gandhi—have had to choose deliberate intellectual paths to achieve success. That's different from the lives of—Helen of Troy, Cleopatra, Marie Antoinette, and Jacqueline Kennedy—the multitudes of women whose beauty guaranteed access to men and to power.

This is something a woman like you can never empathize with because it is something that has never been part of your experience. *(She pauses.)* There? Do you hear that?

ASTORGA. The sounds in the hall?

KIRKPATRICK. Those are not sounds, those are the footsteps of men.

ASTORGA. Men?

KIRKPATRICK. Oh, please. You can't be that naïve. Whenever I'm here in the restroom alone, the hall is as silent as a mausoleum. But whenever you need to take a piss, suddenly it becomes as busy as Grand Central Station. The ambassadors, they prowl, trying to hear what we say, trying to steal a glimpse of you as you come and go. It's to be expected. Men are men, and these men are powerful—and therefore possessed by a sense of entitled lechery.

ASTORGA. You mean this corridor is not always busy?

KIRKPATRICK. No, Nora Oblivious. It isn't!

ASTORGA. They can't possibly be interested in me.

KIRKPATRICK. Of course they are. Are you blind to the way they look at you?

ASTORGA. Well, yes—and no.

KIRKPATRICK. Yes and no. Come now, you know very well what they're thinking, these ambassadors. The British, German, and French ambassadors in particular.

ASTORGA. Really?

KIRKPATRICK. Yes, really.

ASTORGA. What do you suppose goes through their minds?

KIRKPATRICK. My dear, what do you think? You overthrew more than Anastasio Somoza; you overthrew the stereotype of what a woman can or should do. You are a woman warrior who used the power of her sex to slay an enemy general. As such, you are more than a woman, you are a dominatrix. Take the British ambassador, for example. That man wants nothing more than to be lying across your lap while you administer a sound spanking on his bare ass.

ASTORGA. *(Laughing)* You are impossible!

KIRKPATRICK. The British fetish, it's called. That's far different from the German ambassador's longings.

ASTORGA. Which might those be?

KIRKPATRICK. That man? Why, he just fantasies about the possibility of being naked, on his knees, with his hands bound behind his back and you are standing before him, telling him what a bad, bad boy he has been. And then you slap him across the face.

ASTORGA. *(Laughing)* You are preposterous, Ambassador Kirkpatrick!

KIRKPATRICK. I am anything but preposterous. But the German delegate's fantasy pales in comparison to what torments the dreams of the French ambassador.

ASTORGA. That sweet darling of a man?

KIRKPATRICK. My dear, Paris didn't clear the mines from Nicaraguan harbors out of the goodness of the hearts of the French. And Union Square Café was chosen to impress you.

ASTORGA. Tell me. What does the French ambassador want from me?

KIRKPATRICK. Nothing in this world would make that man happier, Nora Astorga, than to have you . . . *fuck him with a dildo!*

Scene 3

The White House, Washington, D.C.

1986. NANCY REAGAN *is in the Oval Office, on her knees. There is a bowl on the floor next to her. She is collecting spilled jellybeans. The door opens and Jeane* KIRKPATRICK *enters.*

KIRKPATRICK. *(Smiling)* You don't have to be down on your knees, Mrs. Reagan. This is Washington, not Hollywood.

NANCY REAGAN. *(Stands up. She holds a bowl of jellybeans in one arm.)* What is that supposed to mean?

KIRKPATRICK. Whatever it is that you think it is supposed to mean.

NANCY REAGAN. No. I want to know what you meant by that remark.

KIRKPATRICK. Did I mention I had a lovely weekend at the Kennedy compound on Martha's Vineyard? Teddy regaled us with tawdry stories Peter Lawford told him about how a B movie actress by the name of Nancy Davis moved up the ladder of the Hollywood establishment—one act of fellatio—at a time.

NANCY REAGAN. *(She moves closer to* KIRKPATRICK, *placing the bowl of jellybeans on a table.)* How dare you speak to me like that! Lawford was a bitter man because I found him . . . inadequate.

KIRKPATRICK. With a mouth as big as yours, I suppose that might be the case.

NANCY REAGAN. *(Moving closer to* KIRKPATRICK) How dare you speak to me this way! My husband is the President of the United States of America!

KIRKPATRICK. A woman whose worth is determined by that of her husband is a woman who has no worth. *(*NANCY REAGAN *slaps* KIRKPATRICK *across the face.* KIRKPATRICK *speaks slowly.)* Blow. Job. Queen.

(NANCY REAGAN *slaps* KIRKPATRICK *across the face again. The door to the restroom opens and* RONALD REAGAN, *holding a damp washcloth he is rubbing on the side of his trousers, enters.*)

RONALD REAGAN. Did I miss anything?

NANCY REAGAN. *(Approaching* RONALD REAGAN, *she takes the washcloth from his hand and wipes it against his trousers.)* No, I think you got it all, Ronnie.

RONALD REAGAN. Those licorice jellybeans always make a mess. *(He looks up and sees* KIRKPATRICK.*)* Oh, Jeane, you're here! Good. *(He addresses* NANCY REAGAN.*)* Mommy, if you please.

(NANCY REAGAN *folds the washcloth as she walks to the door, ignoring* KIRKPATRICK. *She slams the door behind her.*)

RONALD REAGAN. Jeane, I want to thank you for seeing me, especially on such short notice.

KIRKPATRICK. I'm always here for you, Mr. President.

RONALD REAGAN. Good. I don't have to tell you how disappointed I am that the World Court ruled against us. We have been ordered to compensate Nicaragua. Now, I don't blame Vernon or his staff, but I just believe that, somehow, had you been at the U.N., things would have turned out differently.

KIRKPATRICK. There's no way to know, Mr. President.

RONALD REAGAN. Well, this is what I want you to do. I want you to go to New York and help Vernon. I think you can develop a strategy to neutralize that woman, Nora Astorga. Will you do that, Jeane?

KIRKPATRICK. Yes, Mr. President.

(RONALD REAGAN *pulls the handkerchief from his breast pocket and hands it over to* KIRKPATRICK.*)*

RONALD REAGAN. Here, Jeane.

KIRKPATRICK. What's this, Mr. President?

RONALD REAGAN. I think you put on too much rouge on your left cheek; you should wipe some off. I want you to look your best.

Scene 4

Jeane KIRKPATRICK'S *offices at the American Enterprise Institute, Washington, D.C.*

1987. KIRKPATRICK'S *aide, Charles* REYNOLDS, *is at his desk working.* KIRKPATRICK *enters.*

REYNOLDS. You're scheduled to meet with Ambassador Walters again, Professor Kirkpatrick.

KIRKPATRICK. Yes. For more than a year I've been conferring with that idiot and Nora Astorga still keeps besting us, Charles. ¡Qué cosa mas increíble!

REYNOLDS. Your Spanish is sublime!

KIRKPATRICK. Charles, you have known that I'm fluent in Spanish and French?

REYNOLDS. Yes, I've known.

KIRKPATRICK. Then why have you gone along with my little charade?

REYNOLDS. In diplomacy, I learned that one has to go along with make-believe if one is to make-happen.

KIRKPATRICK. Touché, Charles. *(She pauses and smiles.)* Nuance and intelligence in a man is so rare. Are you sure you weren't born female and trans-whatever into a man? You have the common sense of the goddess.

REYNOLDS. Speaking of goddesses, the peh-rrrah is now being compared to Charlotte Corday.

KIRKPATRICK. Who?

REYNOLDS. Marat's killer. Charlotte Corday hoped to put an end to the Reign of Terror in France by killing him. His murder was immortalized by Jacques-Louis David in his painting *La Mort de Marat*. Arrested, she was asked what she had to say in her defense. She answered, "Nothing, except that I have succeeded." She was then sentenced to death by guillotine. That's who they are comparing Nora Astorga to these days, Professor Kirkpatrick. Her myth grows by the day!

KIRKPATRICK. Charles, most altruistic people contemplate

donating their brains to science. I think, however, that you should consider leaving your brain to Trivial Pursuit.

REYNOLDS. Thank you for the suggestion, but may I also suggest that it's time for more Toilet Diplomacy? You know what they say.

KIRKPATRICK. And what would that be, Charles?

REYNOLDS. If at first you don't succeed, try, try again.

KIRKPATRICK. Is that what they say? Then it's more Toilet Diplomacy, Charles.

Scene 5

United Nations, New York.

Nora ASTORGA *is in the women's room brushing her hair and putting on earrings. Jeane* KIRKPATRICK *enters.*

KIRKPATRICK. Half an hour before cocktails begin, I always know where to find you, Ambassador Astorga, getting ready to charm and disarm.

ASTORGA. You're in town? More consultations with Ambassador Walters? God knows Vernon needs guidance, Professor Kirkpatrick.

KIRKPATRICK. I, too, would gloat had I prevailed at the World Court over the United States. Relish the moment—I suspect it will be an isolated victory for Nicaragua.

ASTORGA. We shall see about that.

KIRKPATRICK. Speaking of seeing things, I want to see things as clearly as possible. (KIRKPATRICK *lights a cigarette.*) May I ask certain questions I've had in the back of my mind?

ASTORGA. Ask away.

KIRKPATRICK. I heard the stories, read the media accounts, and been debriefed on the matter. But I am curious about what exactly led you to find yourself working to undermine the Somoza government—and lure an unsuspecting man into your bedroom where he was slain by your accomplices. How did a graduate of Catholic University in Washington, D.C. become the most wanted guerrilla in Latin America?

ASTORGA. That's a fair request, and I will answer you. It happened gradually, and not by design. It was, for me, after graduating from Catholic University, a spiritual and an existential crisis. What was my life to mean? And the more I thought about the life of my country, it was a natural evolution to embrace rebellion against that oppressive regime. I grew to resent the privileged class into which I had been born, had been raised. Mine was a shallow and superficial life. And by that I mean it was a life that benefited no one other than me. The decision to join the struggle against the dictatorship gave me strength and purpose. Of course my life changed. This very good and proper Catholic girl left the church. I saw the church leadership as complicit in the status quo.

KIRKPATRICK. You saw them as giving people food for a day, but not teaching them how to fish for themselves?

ASTORGA. Yes, that's one way of explaining it.

KIRKPATRICK. Your crisis of faith, if it was that, had more to do with the politics of the Catholic Church—or were you anticlerical. After all, your cherished fellow Sandinista and perpetual pain in the ass, Miguel d'Escoto, is a priest. How dare he call Ronald Reagan the butcher of the Nicaraguan people!

ASTORGA. *(She laughs.)* Political rhetoric can be melodramatic and hyperbolic, I don't have to remind you, Conservative Hawk Kirkpatrick.

*(*KIRKPATRICK *laughs, smiling.)*

KIRKPATRICK. The media distort as only the media can distort.

ASTORGA. I became involved with General Reynaldo Pérez Vega as part of my work for justice. At that time I was an attorney at one of the biggest construction companies in Nicaragua. That gave me access. I worked with government officials and also with the National Guard. The general—known as El Perro, or The Dog—was notorious for his corruption and brutality. He had the reputation of being a womanizer and, like men of his class, he felt entitled to any woman he fancied. After my divorce was finalized, I was fair game—his only sense of decency was that he would not seduce a married woman. His fascination with me was well known. My fellow rebels said: "Keep him interested, and we'll tell you when we've analyzed the situation. Let's see what good we can get out of him." That's why I began to flirt with him. When the moment arrived that our plan was finalized, we had to move. "Look," I told him, "you know I'm willing, but it's going to have to be my way. I'm not the sort of woman you're used to dealing with. I'm an independent woman, and I have the right to choose who, where, and when." He quickly accepted this proposition. The original plan was to kidnap him and to exchange him for political prisoners. The plan called for me to make a date with him to come to my house. There would be three compañeros: one in a hallway closet, another in the room opposite the bedroom, and another in a utility closet. I was to disarm him, while he suspected nothing. When he was in bed, completely defenseless, my compañeros would move into action.

KIRKPATRICK. Go on. You are confirming what I thought happened.

ASTORGA. He arrived and all he wanted to do was to get on with it. No drinks or conversation. No foreplay. There was none of the subtlety or delicacy men use from time to time. He just arrived and said, "Here I am. Let's do it." When I suggested a drink, he said, "No, no, no. What for?" Then he followed me into the bedroom. To allay any fear, I began to undress until I was completely naked. Then I walked to him, kissed him, and removed his firearm, jacket and unbuttoned his shirt. He removed his shoes and belt. He was about to take off his trousers, when the compañeros burst into the room and seized him. He put up quite a fight. He began to shout to his bodyguard, but the guard didn't hear him. He resisted too much, and they had to shoot him. His blood soaked into my mattress. I had no choice but to escape with my comrades right then.

KIRKPATRICK. You left and abandoned your daughters who were at your mother's house. I have three sons, and I cannot imagine having the courage to leave them, not knowing what would become of them.

ASTORGA. I had no choice.

KIRKPATRICK. And that's how Nora Astorga became Tanya, a guerrilla, and the most wanted woman in Latin America.

ASTORGA. Do you believe me?

KIRKPATRICK. Yes, I do. But do you consider this murder an accomplishment?

ASTORGA. It is something that I am not proud of, but neither am I ashamed of it. It is what happened and it was an act of revolutionary justice. No more and no less.

KIRKPATRICK. Is this, using your sex, to entrap a man, your greatest accomplishment in life?

ASTORGA. It is an accomplishment, and it belongs to me alone. But the next accomplishment I want is for the President of the United States of America to be forced to address the American people and acknowledge that your government was funding counter revolutionaries waging war on my nation.

(ASTORGA *closes her eyes and leans forward. She places her hands on the sink counter to support herself.* KIRKPATRICK *becomes alarmed.*)

KIRKPATRICK. What's wrong?

ASTORGA. Nothing's wrong.

KIRKPATRICK. Something is wrong, Nora.

ASTORGA. Nothing's wrong . . . I'm fine. I—I don't know—I don't know what's wrong.

(KIRKPATRICK *reaches over and places her hand on* ASTORGA'S *forehead.*

KIRKPATRICK. You don't have a fever. *(She places her hand on* ASTORGA'S *neck.)* Your throat—your collarbone, they are both warm. *(She moves her hand lower, resting on* ASTORGA'S *breast.)* Your breast is warm. You have a localized fever.

ASTORGA. I'm fine, I'll be fine.

KIRKPATRICK. We need to get you to a doctor.

ASTORGA. I'll be fine.

KIRKPATRICK. You listen to me, young woman. Nancy Reagan was diagnosed with breast cancer earlier this year. We need to have you checked out. And now.

ASTORGA. No, I'm fine. It's just nicotine withdrawal—I'm desperate to quit smoking before it kills me. But I'm fine.

KIRKPATRICK. You are not fine, Nora. We have to get you to a doctor. Now!

Scene 6

The White House. Washington, D.C.

RONALD REAGAN *is in the Oval Office. There is a television camera and he is about to speak to the American people.* NANCY REAGAN *is to one side, pacing back and forth.*

KIRKPATRICK *is in her office, watching the broadcast. Nora* ASTORGA *is in her office at the United Nations also watching a television monitor.*

RONALD REAGAN. My fellow Americans: I've spoken to you from this historic office on many occasions and about many things. The power of the Presidency is often thought to reside within this Oval Office. Yet it doesn't rest here; it rests in you, the American people, and in your trust. Your trust is what gives a President his powers of leadership and his personal strength, and it's what I want to talk to you about this evening. For the past three months, I've been silent on the revelations about Iran. Well, the reason I haven't spoken to you before now is this: You deserve the truth. And as frustrating as the waiting has been, I felt it was improper to come to you with sketchy reports, or possibly even erroneous statements, which would then have to be corrected, creating even more doubt and confusion. There's been enough of that. I've paid a price for my silence in terms of your trust and confidence. But I've had to wait, as you have, for the complete story. Let's start with the part that is the most controversial. A few months ago I told the American people I did not trade arms for hostages. My heart and my best intentions still tell me that's true, but the facts and the evidence tell me it is not. As the Tower board reported, what began as a strategic opening to Iran deteriorated, in its implementation, into trading arms for hostages. This runs counter to my own beliefs, to administration policy, and to the original strategy we had in mind. There are reasons why it happened, but no excuses. It was a mistake. Now, another major aspect of the Board's findings regards the transfer of funds to the Nicaraguan Contras. As I told the Tower board, I didn't know about any diversion of funds to the Contras. But as President, I cannot escape responsibility. My fellow Americans, I have a great deal that I want to accomplish with you and for you over the next two years. And the Lord willing, that's exactly what I intend to do. Good night, and God bless you.

(KIRKPATRICK *picks up the telephone and dials. A second later the telephone rings in* ASTORGA'S *office. She picks up the receiver.*)

KIRKPATRICK. My dear, as an American, I am appalled at this monumental failure in our nation's foreign policy. But as a woman, I must commend you on your well-fought and well-earned legal victory exposing those sons of bitches that siphoned monies from the arms sales to fund the Contras fighting your government. You have, alone and through the sheer willpower, managed to make the United Nations into the graveyard of American ambition. That, I must say, is a monumental achievement. One more thing: This conversation never happened.

ASTORGA. Of course this conversation never happened. Most women's achievements, officially, have never happened.

KIRKPATRICK. Stay the course on your radiation and chemotherapy, my dear. You're destined to be a survivor. I know that for certain. Goodnight, Ambassador Astorga.

Scene 7

The White House, Washington, D.C.

RONALD REAGAN *is in the Oval Office, reading a brief. The door opens and* KIRKPATRICK *enters.* RONALD REAGAN *removes his reading glasses and welcomes* KIRKPATRICK.

RONALD REAGAN. *(*RONALD REAGAN *stands up and goes to meet* KIRKPATRICK, *escorting her to a sitting area.)* Oh, Jeane, thank you for coming on such short notice.

KIRKPATRICK. I'm not sure how I can assist Vernon at the United Nations any further than I already have, Mr. President.

RONALD REAGAN. Well, Jeane, I just think that you can help him prevent the General Assembly from voting against the U.S. on this World Court ruling.

KIRKPATRICK. Mr. President, as you know, by refusing to accept the World Court's jurisdiction and complying with the order to compensate Nicaragua, it makes it almost impossible defend our foreign policy.

(The door opens and NANCY REAGAN *is seen. She is not noticed and she stands in the door frame, watching* KIRKPATRICK *and* RONALD REAGAN *speak.)*

RONALD REAGAN. That's just it, Jeane. Vernon tells me that if it came to a vote today, only Israel and El Salvador would vote with us—every other nation would demand we compensate the Sandinistas. I don't understand why the world community is against us. What does Secretary-General Pérez de Cuéllar have to say?

KIRKPATRICK. Pérez de Cuéllar says that if the U.S. does not agree to full and immediate compliance, then we will become an outlaw nation. The world believes the U.S. is contributing to increasing disorder.

RONALD REAGAN. Is that what he says?

KIRKPATRICK. Yes, Mr. President.

RONALD REAGAN. Our ideal as a nation where the rule of law prevails has to be defended, Jeane. I want you to go to New York and help Vernon out.

KIRKPATRICK. Yes, Mr. President. I'll leave tomorrow morning.

RONALD REAGAN. Good.

KIRKPATRICK. Is that all, Mr. President?

(RONALD REAGAN *pauses, looking confused. Then he speaks.*)

RONALD REAGAN. Yes . . . uh, Jeane . . . What does Secretary-General Pérez de Cuéllar have to say?

KIRKPATRICK. About what?

RONALD REAGAN. What does Secretary-General Pérez de Cuéllar have to say about our complying with the World Court ruling against us?

(KIRKPATRICK *pauses and studies* RONALD REAGAN.)

KIRKPATRICK. You just asked me that a moment ago. And I answered. Don't you remember, Mr. President?

RONALD REAGAN. I did?

KIRKPATRICK. Yes, and I replied that he demanded our full and immediate compliance with the World Court's order. Don't you remember?

(RONALD REAGAN *is confused.*)

RONALD REAGAN. I don't know. I don't know if I remember having asked you that.

KIRKPATRICK. Well, it's not important. I'll go to New York tomorrow and work to prevent the General Assembly from voting against us, Mr. President. (KIRKPATRICK *stands and sees* NANCY REAGAN *in the door frame.*) Good night, Mr. President.

(RONALD REAGAN *says nothing.* KIRKPATRICK *walks to the open door. She stops when she nears* NANCY REAGAN.)

NANCY REAGAN. *(Softly, to* KIRKPATRICK*)* Now you know. And if you say a word about this to anyone, you'll have to answer to me.

(KIRKPATRICK *exits.* NANCY REAGAN *enters the Oval Office and closes the door behind her.* RONALD REAGAN *notices her.*)

RONALD REAGAN. Oh, Mommy, there you are.

NANCY REAGAN. Of course I'm here!

RONALD REAGAN. Well, you can't stay long. I'm meeting with

Jeane Kirkpatrick shortly. And I know you have a thing going on with her.

NANCY REAGAN. Oh, Ronnie, don't worry. I'll behave myself.

RONALD REAGAN. Do you promise to watch yourself? I don't want to have to worry about anything.

(NANCY REAGAN *walks to the desk and embraces* RONALD REAGAN, *kissing him.*)

NANCY REAGAN. You don't have to worry about anything. Not a single thing, my darling husband.

Scene 8

United Nations, New York.

Carlos GONZÁLEZ *sits at his desk doing paperwork. Jeane* KIRKPATRICK, *angered and determined, enters.*

KIRKPATRICK. Where is she? The General Assembly just voted 94 to 3 to condemn the United States. November 12, 1987 will be remembered as an outrage. She masterminded this vote, manipulating all the fucking pricks-for-ambassadors that plague this place! Where is she?

GONZÁLEZ. She who?

KIRKPATRICK. Who do you think? Cinderella and your nation's ambassador.

GONZÁLEZ. *(Unfazed)* Neither is here.

KIRKPATRICK. I didn't expect Cinderella to be here, but where is Nora Astorga? *(She looks around and notices the bouquets of flowers; she calms down.)* What's with all the flowers? I don't know if this office looks more like a florist shop or a funeral home.

GONZÁLEZ. You don't know then?

KIRKPATRICK. Know what?

GONZÁLEZ. She has been hospitalized.

KIRKPATRICK. What?

GONZÁLEZ. Two days ago.

KIRKPATRICK. What happened?

GONZÁLEZ. Everything was fine—until it wasn't.

KIRKPATRICK. Can you be less ambiguous?

GONZÁLEZ. She was fine two days ago. Then she felt faint, had a fever, and she collapsed while working right there at her desk.

KIRKPATRICK. What?

GONZÁLEZ. Her cancer has returned.

KIRKPATRICK. Does she have adequate doctors?

GONZÁLEZ. Dr. Kevin Cahill is her physician. One of the best in this city.

KIRKPATRICK. I came up here to confer with Ambassador Walters for the afternoon and watch the vote. I planned to return to Washington this evening. But I want to see her. If I have to stay overnight, then that's what I'll have to do.

GONZÁLEZ. That would be wise, if you want to see her. Her deputy, Julio Icaza, is now acting in her stead. And, you see, I'm making arrangements for an air ambulance to take her home.

KIRKPATRICK. Home?

GONZÁLEZ. Those are her wishes. Her plane won't be able to fly higher than 7,000 feet above sea level; she's too weak to withstand a pressurized cabin. Dr. Cahill will be with her to monitor her vitals. She wants to go home.

KIRKPATRICK. Home? (KIRKPATRICK, *disoriented, walks around looking at the bouquets of flowers.*) France. Germany. Spain. Mexico. Japan. Saudi Arabia. India. Kenya. Argentina. Canada. Italy. Brazil. Cuba. Korea. (*She motions at the other bouquets of flowers.*) Etcetera, etcetera, etcetera. They all wish her well. The whole world wishes her well.

GONZÁLEZ. She is much admired.

KIRKPATRICK. Home, you said? An air ambulance? Back to Nicaragua?

GONZÁLEZ. Yes.

KIRKPATRICK. (*In a soft, tender manner*) But why? The United Nations *is* her home.

Scene 9

Jeane KIRKPATRICK'S *offices at the American Enterprise Institute, Washington, D.C.*

1988. KIRKPATRICK'S *aide, Charles* REYNOLDS, *enters, carrying a vase with red roses. He places them on* KIRKPATRICK'S *desk. He proceeds to turn on the computers in the room before sitting at his desk to begin work.* KIRKPATRICK *enters.*

REYNOLDS. Good morning, Professor Kirkpatrick.

KIRKPATRICK. Of course. And the same to you, Charles. *(She points across her office.)* What are those roses on my desk for?

REYNOLDS. It's Valentine's Day. They're from your husband, Evron.

KIRKPATRICK. Oh, dear, I suppose I'll have to send him something! I always forget these dates, but I just can't let my mind get cluttered up with bullshit holidays.

REYNOLDS. And bullshit it is!

KIRKPATRICK. No one sent you anything, I take it?

(The telephone rings and REYNOLDS *answers it.)*

REYNOLDS. Professor Kirkpatrick's office. *(Pause.)* I see. *(Pause.)* In about twenty minutes they'll release a statement? I got it. Thank you for calling. No, no, don't worry. She's right here. I'll let her know.

KIRKPATRICK. Know what?

REYNOLDS. It's about that bitch.

KIRKPATRICK. Which bitch? There are so many in my life.

REYNOLDS. It's the peh-rrrah.

KIRKPATRICK. Nora Astorga?

REYNOLDS. Yes, that bitch.

*(*KIRKPATRICK *walks over to her desk, reaches for a red rose, sits down, and brings the rose to her nostrils as she speaks.)*

KIRKPATRICK. Charles, I'm only going to say this once, so listen up. Nora Astorga, to you, to me, and to everyone else on this planet is Her Excellency. Got that?

REYNOLDS. Yes. Understood.

KIRKPATRICK. Now, what were you going to say?

REYNOLDS. *(He hesitates, then speaks slowly.)* Her Excellency died about twenty minutes ago. The hospital in Managua is going to issue a statement to the press at the top of the hour.

KIRKPATRICK. Died?

REYNOLDS. She lost her battle against cancer.

KIRKPATRICK. Oh, no, it can't be. That brave, beautiful girl. *(She pauses as she puts the rose down, pricking her finger on a thorn.)* How old was she?

REYNOLDS. She turned thirty-nine just two months ago.

KIRKPATRICK. Thirty-nine. She had her whole life ahead of her. And we, humanity, are now robbed of her presence!

REYNOLDS. When did you speak to her last?

KIRKPATRICK. Around Christmastime, Charles. She told me how, when they arrived in Managua, they opened the door, but it took her twenty minutes to disembark. She made Dr. Cahill find her lipstick. She brushed her hair and insisted that she walk off the plane on her own.

REYNOLDS. Well, if it's any consolation, you know what they say.

KIRKPATRICK. *(Irritated)* No, Charles, what do they say in these situations? In the face of such cruel fate?

REYNOLDS. Only the good die young.

KIRKPATRICK. Is that the pathetic platitude they say?

REYNOLDS. Yes, it is.

KIRKPATRICK. Well, I suppose if that's the case, Charles, then I can look forward to a very, very, very long life.

BLACKOUT

END OF PLAY